In the treasure of culinary culture, Viet Nam is home to a wide variety of gourmet dishes, from daily folk dishes to casual cuisine to serve festivals and the family with their own looks. Each of the domain regions on the country has different dishes and brings separate meanings that make up the identity of each nation. It reflects the tradition and specificity of every resident living in each area. So learn about the food of some peoples in the community of Vietnamese peoples not only to know about the food characteristics that through which to understand the belief, the culture and the typical features of each class of residents.

Affordable beauty of Vietnamese culinary culture has begun from such casual things. From the stub, Vietnamese people have been the owner of the Red River Culture, which highlights the rice civilization. Although living in the plains, neutral or in mountainous valleys, Lac Viet people are still sticking to rice trees and maintaining life-planting, settling. In order to ensure a high-strength of water in harsh areas, from the old-fashioned gluteal, the Mongolian community has noticed irrigation, leveraging the power of nature to sustain his life. Along with the time, today's daily glutinous, dining of the tall buttock people also have many changes, though that the plants in everyday life are taken from nature or by the hands of the labour hand, but the way food is processed and other , a more demanding calculation. From food demand to enough food, it is now a need to enjoy food. In daily dishes as well as festivals, they are very important to spice and color because of the natural features here in cold prices, which require warm, hot food with strong colours. If the day's dining is usually a real requirement, make sure the no need is at the frozen bazaars, the needs of eating sympathy are placed on top. Just a bottle of wine and a pan of victory, in turn, each person will drink generic bowls of wine and eat a pan of soup. It's a beautiful picture of the community

and equality of the buttocks, the knife in the very high way of eating. Especially they are very important to the rich color of the dish.

Chapter I

Vietnamese and present cuisine

Vietnam's culinary culture is compact in two "*know-how*", hidden in which the art and beauty in the culture of conduct. So new to "*eat the pot, sit in the direction*", by passing the food that the guess knows from the characteristic to the way, the academic level of the person eating.

The beauty of Vietnamese culinary culture originates from the main marker of the rice agrarian platform. Despite the oneness, the family or the party, the Vietnamese menu can not lack rice-crops. Vietnamese proverbs: "*People who live on rice, fish on water* "; "*Boring mother's gut*"; Or, "*to crave for cravings, not boring, all roads*" The culture of agriculture has dominated the Vietnamese flora and fauna structure. Vietnamese meals may lack meat, fish, but can not lack vegetables, berries by: *"Eating non-vegetables such as rich dead" empty "*; "Eat no vegetables like fighting no more people"...

Vietnamese dishes If only one dish is difficult to call the rice, and only one person sitting in food is also difficult to feel the good of each dish. The integrity and integrity of this community has become the most unique beauty in Vietnamese culinary culture. If the Westerners enjoy the analytical style, eat all the dishes and then move the other dishes, the Vietnamese rice will ever be generous with all the items cleaned up at the same time: *any rice , any vegetables, any meat, any fish, more bowls of baby sauce...* It is possible to say, each Vietnamese dish has converged in the synthesis of the processing: it is completely boiled in stir fried, rening, Qin, steaming..., so that harmonize hot-cold, negative elements. The colds must eat ginger porridge, the sunshine must eat the porridge. Folk we save no

less the knife talks about how to synthessum the ingredients when cooking Vietnamese people: "*cooked bong with dry* " Dead oil on the grave is also up for food "; "*vegetables cooked with syrup. Ginger Jasmine a slice for her husband* "; Or "*drop each other in the crab pool* " I'm about to cook yogurt in the woods. Sitting in front of the rice rolls, the Vietnamese can select the same as preference dishes to enjoy, the senses are also at the same time to feel the food: the nose can smell the smell of fresh, the eye can see the colours , the tongue can taste typical flavors. As such, the whole meal is a general process, each bowl of rice, each rice piece is the result of that synthetic process.

Going close, going away, we still try to get back home to the house with a family of dark rice. Despite being late, late, the people in the House are still waiting to have enough new member to use the rice. Any party, the meeting can not take place but only one person. This is because in culinary culture, Vietnamese people always treat the community. If the western person every single user has a disk, a place where the convenience is completed, the Vietnamese must take the pants, around the new rice-eating. With the Vietnamese, the time of eating is for people to carry out cultural communication, together with face, chat, capture information about the lives of each other. and the main dining space is the place to closely close the relationships between persons of the family, in addition to society. As a result, the dishes on the berry can be eaten, who are not depending on the interests, but the rice cooker and the sauce is a community dish that the people who sit around the wheels are also used. and chopsticks – unique inindispensable widgets while eating the Vietnamese are the most versatile means of connecting the arms, helping the people around the parachutes, sitting in the distance, are still in the same way that the food can be used on the raspberry and everyone else.

Despite having spent a thousand years in writing, many different periods of history, at the time of the rise, but the inner essence of the Vietnamese Mon's food is still there. Always be a separate, unique, human-specific compression. The essence of the flower has printed in the long every Vietnamese people. Although society has evolved, the Vietnamese have been present in five continents, four seas, but no matter where to go, Vietnamese people are always giving themselves the same ethnic identity. They are always very angry and promoted to the Vietnamese national identity.

Speaking to the country of Vietnam often remember to have hue beef bun, pho, cake roll... but that's just a small part of a chain of Vietnamese dishes from the sack. Contrary to the different stages of Vietnamese history again create strange dishes, but in particular, it is always the nature of Vietnamese people, always bold Vietnamese identity.

Chapter II

Vietnamese featured Dishes

Vietnam, with a rich and abundant culinary culture, Vietnam's culinary background left the impression for many foreign visitors. Vietnamese dishes are gradually confirmed in the hearts of international tourists, here are the world's most popular Vietnamese dishes.

I. Bread.

Honored as one of the most delicious street dishes in the world, Vietnamese burgers are selected, this is a fascinating dish not only with international visitors but also the favorite Vietnamese cuisine.

Vietnamese bread brand in recent years is becoming popular everywhere, from Asia, Europe to Australia, USA... known as one of the world's favourite street dishes, the bread or "Vietnamese bread" gradually Standing in the village of global food.

As with the Westerners, the bread is the main dish, then in Vietnam, the bread is simply like a dish playing or used to eat breakfast when people don't have much time. Introduced to Vietnam from the French occupation, the main bread was the interference between the two French-Vietnamese culinary cultures. Over time, how as well as the recipe of processing material ingredients for human bread is also gradually changed, "free" and different according to the specific cuisine of each domain.

Eating bread-do not know when the person has become the hobby of many, many generations. From the elderly to children, from male to female, if the Vietnamese are sure everyone has to enjoy the bread dish at least once in life. Therefore, it is not even to say that bread is the most intimate dish of all walks, because it is easy to eat and is also easy to "ghiben"-regardless of the class bread or the floury bread. In particular, the bread car is one of the most easily caught things when you set your feet to any province, in Vietnam.

Just off from the 10,000-15,000 bronze is that you have on hand a bread drive to "gnaw" delectable. Also because of his overstanding, Vietnamese people go away often or remember the taste of home bread. Sandwiches or baguettes – although also the bread, also aromatic, is also delicious, but it is naturally impossible to replace the traditional, familiar Vietnamese bread flavor. This has created motivation for many to stand out self-establishment of the goods, the free bread sale where the guests land.

From then on, "selling bread" was born, not the creation of stable jobs for many Vietnamese people from home but also a great way to promote Vietnamese cuisine, contributing to a Vietnamese food to the world community. Today, foreigners know more bread, even the name "bread" is also officially present in the Oxford-marked dictionary of Vietnam which adds a recognized dish in the village of World food beside "pho". Many well-known journalists and talented chefs also therefore come to Vietnam to find out for the most delicious planetary bread seats. They must be sampled once in their lives.

Street food can't be missing bread, in Saigon too. The bread paradise in this city has a multitude of attractive kinds of personality from all kinds of rolls, lagoons, chicken, meat, canned fish, eggs... Not one that constantly has a few recent years of free bread especially the Saigon bread is accustomed to the name for the list of the best street delicacies in the world due to prestige magazines such as Lonely Planet , CNN, Telegraph, National Geographic, BBC... vote. The Saigon bread is attractive to a multitude of variations and it seems that this creation has never stopped.

Although there is a multitude of attractive choices, but the key to a delicious bread drive is also located at the bread drive. These bread drives are extremely soft before the sale is baked in the oven beside, so that you get the crunchy feeling soluble in the mouth every bite a piece. The Saigon bread is particularly in place not only an individual but also generously stuffed into that mixture of salads,vegetables,crispy pickle, aromatic.

1. Bread rolls

Not only the type of human-feeding PA, cold meat, crispy silk pieces are served as a separate dish. In order for guests to fully feel the taste of silk leaf packs, banana rolls are usually not for more raw materials but only subtle little salt spots salty. The Saigon people who crave this dish can stop any of the bread cars.

Apart from silk rolls, the Saigon is also gradually conquered by aromatic flavors, Dai, the slumpy of the cows, a specialty of the Da Nang specialties. Not only shall, many places also for the more African onions, the PA, the cheeseburger to drive the bread of a cow. Extremely attractive.

2. Omelette eggs.

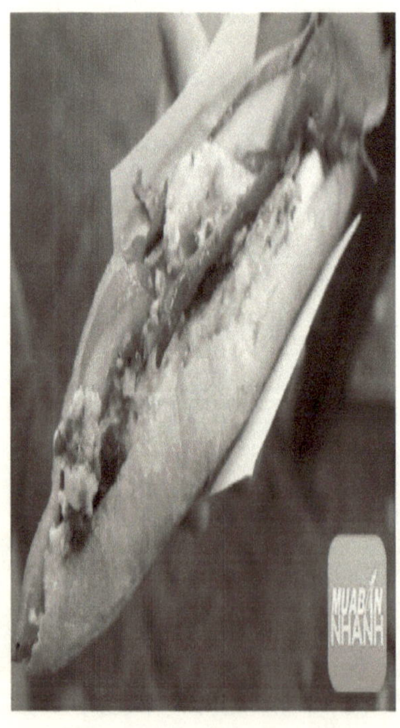

Fried eggs on small cast iron pans such as sharp layers, half-life half-ripe yolk, eaten with pickles, soy sauce, soy sauce... is also one of the favorite types of Saigon bread. In addition to a man's egg, many people prefer to make a plate with the meat, tiny, numb...

Due to simple processing, the tiling bread is present in most of the bakery. But, with the faithful of the pan-fried bread, the high road bread is considered to be the "gut" address.

3. *Grilled Fish*

It's not a good thing not to say that Saigon is not. The proof is that the seafood specialties of the sea are also introduced and gradually become one of the favorite types of bread made by Saigon.

The aromatic bread wheel rolls The fragrant fish that are finished fried, adding a little onions, pickles, some lettuce, chili sauce. The aroma of the fried fish rolls that are attractive to the point of pass can also recognize the appearance of this delicious dish. In addition to those street bread, bakery shop on Bui Thi Xuan Street, or Pasteur Road bakery-The Bien Phu is the familiar venue you can refer to when you want to enjoy a fish sandwich.

4. Chicken Bread Torn

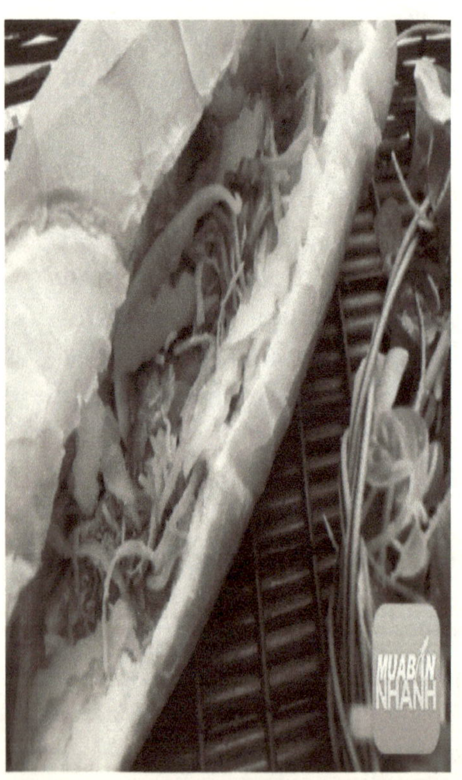

In addition to fish, pork... Chicken is also the material as the favorite bread worker. The chicken tore the yarn, after the taste tasting was roasted on the hot pan for slightly sandwiched with spikes, onion leaves, cucumber... making a delicious bread.

5. Bread

The little people are familiar but delicious, just a few places. A nice little reporter must have a fatty aroma, just right from a half-lean minced meat. Eating breads must also ensure that the hot crispy so that the person on the food can sense enough full of the harmony of the fatty aroma, crispy melt bread where the tongue head.

6. Barbecue

Not only the Vietnamese but also foreign guests have to admit that barbecue sandwiches have a great suction flavor. The food usually must recognize that the appetite of a barbecue drive is located in the balance between the taste, the aroma of the barbecue, the characteristic gentle sweetness of soy sauce, the Sour, cucumber, and slightly spicy.

7. Pa Cold meat.

It is possible to see the bread sandwich, ham is the most delicious main bakery in the matter. In popularity to ten, the car and a glass of bread sold, there are also up to eight bars of bread with butter, numb, ham, cold meat... stuffed vegetables filled with cake.

8. Roast PORK

The pork is a fragrant, fertile, gion, crispy in the hot bread and sliced cucumber, sour, chilli, chili sauce, and is also a favorite bread version in Vietnam.

9. *Pork Dermatome*

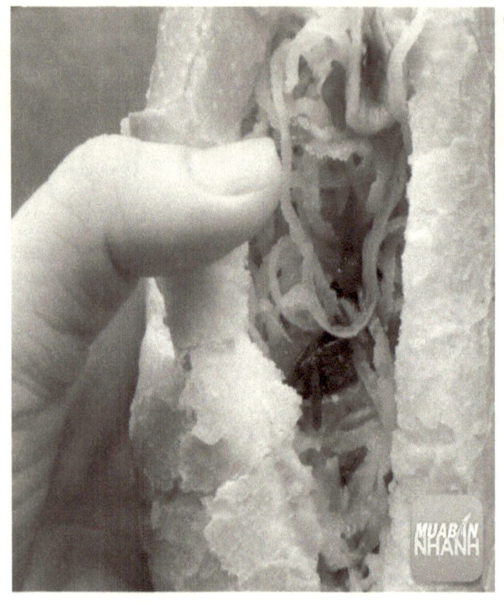

The envelope is not only a delicious dish of rice sheets but also combines very "charm" with bread. In order to increase the attractiveness of the aromatic hearing mixing, the seller usually has to apply the water mix of Chan, the fish sauce to the bold, and then add a few slices of cucumber, sour.

II. Cake Roll.

This dish is no stranger to the Vietnamese, for the guests who each enjoy a cake with the special. The cake roll will have the aroma of aromatic rice eaten with fragrant vegetables and sauces that bring very special flavor.

When the cakes come from, where's the origin, it's not possible to explain. In Hanoi, this is really a pancake for adding a fresh, fleshy-fried, onion-lit wedge and tasty fish sauce with a sausage. Out of Hue, the pancake is the aromatic yellow grilled meat in the water (soy sauce), which is known as the barbecue cake. And then he's wet shrimp, thin cakes, sprinkle shrimp, roll back. I still see the middle-fed women who are not eating, wedge sauce or a minced sauce of chili oil at the very heart of a good compliment.

1. Hanoi Butcher Pie.

Baking powder is the rice that is grind wet so very smooth. After having been made ripe by the steam, the cake leaves will be swept to the flesh, and moc mushrooms and sandalwood has been made ripe. After that, the bakery will use the same cake-making bamboo, which has four shorter tracks and presents to the disc. After folding the first turn on the disc, a little rusnail shrimp will be sprinkled on the pancake pads and on the same point some aromatic vegetables such as peppermint, coriander... The cake will be enjoyed with the bowl of sauce with a few slices and little onions in it.

2. Egg cake.

Lang Son's egg cake only includes chicken eggs and a lean meat, which is rubs into small fibers and water broth is the water that is electronized from the bone and adds spices, onions, odor, pepper, chili.

Many restaurants also use a warehouse of meat for more bold. Chicken eggs are steamed inside the cake leaves, ripe enough to form a thin membrane around the yolk, helping the eggs not be broken. When enjoying, the user will skillfully put a piece of cake into the mouth so that the egg yolk breaks out in the mouth, reconcached with the meat sauce and the well-cleaned, hot and delicious treasures of meat.

This dish requires very hard-to-bakery techniques. The powder is spread out and then closes the lid, waiting for the cooked cake to open the lid and knock the eggs up the cake layer. The one or the smarts are the Doughman who has to cap back and confine at the white layers and stick to the bakery, and the yolk is ripe to the level of training into thin layers that help the egg not be , the new open lid. And then use chopsticks to split the cake into two pieces, skillfully rolled the cake back inside the egg.

III. The food

The food is a variety of distinctive and attractive flavors. The special thing in the bowl is that the water is used, with a spicy, fresh water that gives a special flavor to the food.

1. Rice type

Often appearing in streets, small alleys on the level of either afternoon or shine or even midnight, the times when people are not going to work, go to school... The seller will have an "employee" strolling around the track path according to a percussion set of "Cup". It's a very typical percussion that anyone who hears is going to understand, the customers who want to call the food-out of the detector, and just in a momentarily, the hot, warm-hearted jar will be left to the house.

2. *Fish Rice*

This is a rare type of man known in Saigon, Song is one of the oldest types. However, the same way to cook water from the basement, but this dish is especially because the main ingredients are the most delicious fresh fish, eating with a layer of fatty leopard that forms a protein that is still a characteristic bold.

IV. Fish Storage

The dish is fascinating, with the unscented cooking of fish, soft fish and meat, the traditional treasures that are shed by the land as a special flavor to the food. Manyvisitors to Vietnam have all been in need at least once eaten by a fish meal at once.

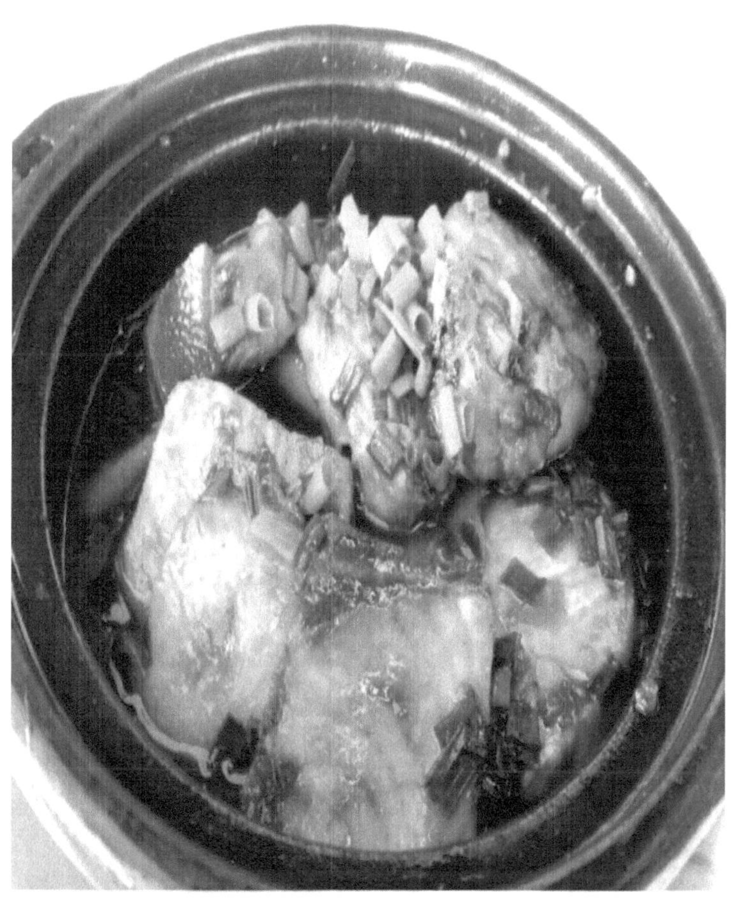

V. Bun Beef Hue

This is probably the most widely selected dish to the central region especially in hue, with a characteristic taste of the urban land, with the sweetness of bone, soft sausage meat, rice vermicelli to conquer any customer not only fo the Vietnamese But also with international guests.

Rice vermicelli is one of the specialties of Hue country, although the vermicelli is also available. In Hue, this is called simply *"rice vermicelli."* Other localities called the "rice vermicelli" for only the origin of this dish. The dish has a main raw material, bun, beef, pork sausage, and a distinctive red-water color. Sometimes the bun is also added to re-beef, crab rolls, and other ingredients depending on the hobby of the cook.

In the water used by bun, the hue usually wedge into a few rugfish sauce, contributing to the very own taste of hue rice vermicelli. After the bone is ripe, it is often added to a few pork rolls or crab-less. Beef can be thinly sliced, embedded in the water used to boil before giving in to the bun (*called the RE beef*). It is also often used to add a little chili powder and spice into the bun and eat with the raw vegetables that include the price, aroma, salads, baby vegetables, chopped banana corn.

VI. Recffled HA NOI

Familiar dishes for foreign visitors to Vietnam. Beef Noodle always delivers a particularly delicate taste and is one of the most impressive dishes with international visitors.

Pho is most famous for the Vietnamese pho Hanoi. Not knowing how to ever, Pho has become an incredibly attractive dish every time you arrive in Hanoi. With a unique flavor that does not have a place to be, Pho Ha Noi has a deep print into the human subconscious, by default it is the most delicious dish. You want to eat noodle right in Hanoi. In the years 1940. Pho was very well known in Hanoi. Pho is a dish that can be eaten on any length of time that you want: morning, lunch, afternoon, dinner. In special points, noodle is not eaten, with anything else. A bowl of noodle soup includes: water, noodle, spices such as pepper, onion leaves, lemon tile, chili... The juice of the noodle can be processed from the beef bones: The bone, the bone and the bone. Bread must be tough, soft. Onion leaves, chili peppers, increased flavor of bowl pho. Depending on the cooking secrets that each place has flavor of different noodle.

There are three main noodle dishes: pho water, stir fried pho and pan. Of the above three types, water noodle is the most popular. The water noodle is eaten hot. A hot and comfortable noodle soup is suitable for frozen days in Hanoi. Water noodle includes beef noodle, chicken noodle, liver noodle. There are different types of noodle that are used by water with different meats. But the gourmet people still choose beef noodle for his menu. Pho dish is attractive by the quintessential and sweet flavor that the water has to offer. Guests are intrigued by Pho food because of its strangeness and unique taste. A fine pho bowl is always present in the porcelain bowl with moderate magnitude. When eating pho, one hand will take chopsticks, the other hand will hold spoons. Chopsticks are most commonly used to eat pho is the bamboo chopstick because of the convenience as well as not smooth dropping noodle bread pieces. Hot noodle soup and no more meals, other beverages. Pho is exquisite cuisine, characterized by the land of Ha A. The noodle soup has made a great understanding of the writers ' generation so that the works are excellent.

Attractive cuisine is famous for both international travelers, each with a journey to Vietnam that offers special things for guests to enjoy Vietnamese cuisine.

Different dishes with different features of the domain floor on the text of the land. These are still the strokes of the free dish, the distinctive, the nature, the only one and only Vietnamese. Vietnamese people are proud of our years, we, Vietnamese people love people, speaking to Vietnam to come up with a special dish where there is no place.

At the next book the author sends the price reading to the real way to cook the free food at home, catering to your beloved little family.

Thank you for reading the price of books!!! See you on the next book...